D1606950

How to Draw the Life and Times of
James Madison

Roderic Schmidt

The Rosen Publishing Group's
PowerKids Press™
New York

To Magdalena

Published in 2006 by The Rosen Publishing Group, Inc.
29 East 21st Street, New York, NY 10010

First Edition

Editors: Melissa Acevedo and Orli Zuravicky
Layout Design: Albert B. Hanner

Illustrations: Cover and Inside by Holly Cefrey

Photo credits: p. 4 Library of Congress Rare Book and Special Collections Division; pp. 7, 24 (top) © Bettmann/Corbis; p. 8 © Carl & Ann Purcell/Corbis; p.9 Courtesy of James Madison University; p. 10 © Corbis; p.12 Courtesy of the Library of Virginia; p. 14 © AP/Wide World Photos; p. 16 Newspaper Collections, State Historical Society of Wisconsin, Madison; p. 18 National Archives and Records Administration; p. 20 Clements Library, University of Michigan; p. 22 White House Historical Association (White House Collection)(123); p. 24 (bottom) © Audrey Gibson/Corbis; p. 26 © Reunion des Musees Nationaux/Art Resources, NY; p. 28 Charles Willson Peale, "James Madison", from the collection of Gilcrease Museum, Tulsa, Oklahoma.

Library of Congress Cataloging-in-Publication Data

Schmidt, Roderic.
How to draw the life and times of James Madison / Roderic Schmidt.
    p. cm. — (A kid's guide to drawing the presidents of the United States of America)
Includes bibliographical references and index.
ISBN 1-4042-2981-7 (library binding)
1. Madison, James, 1751–1836—Juvenile literature. 2. Presidents—United States—Biography—Juvenile literature. 3. Drawing—Technique—Juvenile literature. I. Title. II. Series.

E342.S36 2006
973.5'1'092—dc22

2004014516

Manufactured in the United States of America

Contents

Young James Madison

James Madison was the Father of the Constitution and the fourth president of the United States. He was born in Virginia on March 16, 1751. His parents were wealthy plantation owners. Young James was a small, sickly boy. Though his body was weak, he was very smart. James learned much about life from watching his father manage the family's large plantation. James learned how hard it was to run a large household and farm well. He also learned how to be organized and how to plan ahead. James thought very highly of his father. When James was a young boy, his mother taught him to read and write. Afterward he studied with private teachers and at the nearby school until he went to college. In 1769, Madison started college in New Jersey. After college Madison became involved in government. In 1775, the American Revolution began. The colonies had declared themselves independent from Britain and had begun creating new governments. Though Madison was unable to fight in the revolution because of his poor health, he was active in Virginia's politics and helped create Virginia's new constitution. During the revolution the colonies created a national government with the Articles of Confederation. In 1783, America won the war. Shortly after the war ended, it became clear that this new government was not working well. Madison helped write a new plan of government called the Constitution. He also worked hard to get it ratified. Afterward he became a member of the new country's Congress. Madison then served as President Thomas Jefferson's secretary of state for eight years. Madison was elected president in 1808.

You will need the following supplies to draw the life and times of James Madison:

✓ A sketch pad   ✓ An eraser   ✓ A pencil   ✓ A ruler

These are some of the shapes and drawing terms you need to know:

Horizontal Line	——	Squiggly Line	⌇
Oval	⬭	Trapezoid	⏢
Rectangle	▭	Triangle	△
Shading	▰	Vertical Line	|
Slanted Line	/	Wavy Line	∿

President of the United States

James Madison was inaugurated as president of the United States on March 4, 1809. James and his wife, Dolley, moved to Washington, D.C., the nation's capital. They joined in Washington's social life right away and were popular. They threw parties at which different types of people would meet and talk.

During Madison's presidency, France was fighting a series of wars called the Napoleonic Wars with European countries, mainly with England. During his first years in office, Madison tried to keep America out of the war. However, by the end of his first term, America did get involved. America fought England once more, in what became known as the War of 1812. Though the war did not go well at first, some great naval victories gave Madison enough support to get reelected in 1812. During his second term, the war continued. In 1814, the war ended. Madison was regarded as a hero for standing up to England. In 1817, Madison retired to his home, Montpelier, in Virginia, to farm, write, and host parties with Dolley.

During the War of 1812, the English entered the nation's capital and set fire to many of the buildings. The White House also caught fire. At the time Dolley Madison was at home. This painting shows Dolley saving the Declaration of Independence from the fire.

Madison's Virginia

James Madison's home, Montpelier, in Virginia was built around 1723 by his grandfather.

Map of the United States of America

When James Madison was born, Virginia was one of the wealthiest and most-populated colonies. Many Virginians made their money growing tobacco on the colony's rich farmland. Tobacco was a popular crop in those times, because it could be sold to England for great profit. Virginians farmed tobacco on large plantations that were spread out all over the colony.

Madison grew up in Orange County on a large plantation called Montpelier. About 150 people lived at Montpelier, including slaves, servants, and family. Visitors were always coming and going, too. Madison enjoyed living there. Today Montpelier is being restored to look as it did when James and

Dolley lived there, during the 1820s. Visitors can take tours of Montpelier. They can see the Madisons' dining room and Dolley Madison's bedroom, as well as special exhibits, which include furniture and some of the Madisons' belongings.

The people of Virginia are very proud of their state's history. Orange County, Virginia, has dedicated an entire museum to Madison's life where many of his favorite personal items and papers are on display.

This bronze statue of Madison, created by Lee Leuing and Sherri Treeby, has stood on the grounds of James Madison University since 2002.

James Madison University, located in Harrisonburg, Virginia, serves as the home of the James Madison Center. The James Madison Center is dedicated to collecting information on the life and times of James Madison. In an effort to continue Madison's love of and commitment to education, the center organizes programs, classes, and job opportunities for teachers, students, and members of the community.

A University Education

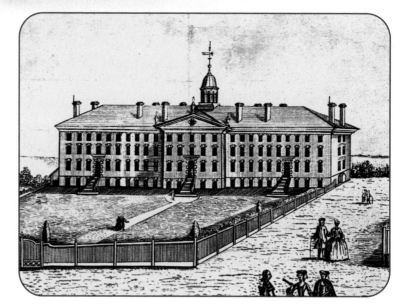

In 1769, James Madison went to the College of New Jersey, which later became Princeton University. He lived in Nassau Hall, a building on the college's grounds. Madison was intelligent. He studied many subjects, including science and languages. He finished his four-year degree in two years, but he used the extra time to study more with the university's president.

It was unusual in those times for the son of a wealthy Virginian plantation owner to attend an out-of-state school, but Madison's father wanted the best education for his son. At Princeton Madison studied with people from different colonies, many of whom practiced different types of Christianity. These experiences would make Madison work very hard later in his life to make sure that people were free to practice religion as they saw fit. In 1772, Madison went back to Virginia, where he became involved in government.

1

You are going to learn to draw Nassau Hall. Begin by drawing a large rectangle. Draw a square in the center of the rectangle. Notice that the bottom line of the square is drawn a bit below the bottom of the rectangle.

2

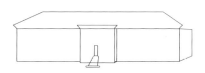

Draw straight lines for the roof as shown. Connect the roof to the rectangle's top corners. Draw the door and entryway in the square as shown. Add lines to the square and to the side of the rectangle as shown.

3

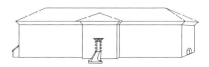

Erase extra lines. Add lines and an upside-down *V* to the roof. Add two lines to the entryway and eight small squares to the sides of the door. Add the shape above the door and the shapes on either side of the building.

4

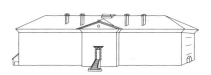

Add lines to the right side of the building. Add lines to the shape on the left. Add the stairs and lines to the entry. Add lines and a circle to the triangle. Draw four chimneys and the lines for the base of the tower on the roof as shown.

5

Erase extra lines. Draw four more chimneys. Add four lines to the rooftop for chimney tops. Draw the body of the tower. Add lines to the triangle. Add windows to the right side of the hall. Draw two more entryways.

6

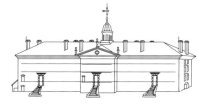

Erase extra lines. Add horizontal lines to the front and the roof of the hall. Add three more lines in the center square. Begin adding the windows. Draw shapes on the roof and tower. Add lines on the right side.

7

Finish drawing the rest of the windows until the front of the hall is covered. Draw a small horizontal line at the bottom of the tower and another one at the bottom of the right side of the hall.

8

Erase extra lines. Finish your building by shading in the windows, doorways, and other parts. Some parts will be darker than the others. Your drawing of Nassau Hall looks great!

Virginian Legislator

In 1776, James Madison attended the Virginia Convention at the statehouse, shown above, in Virginia's former capital, Williamsburg. It was there that representatives created a new constitution for Virginia. The constitution outlined a government run by elected citizens who would govern fairly. Virginia's Declaration of Rights outlined citizens' individual rights and vowed to protect these rights. Madison worked on the part of the declaration about religion. During that time kings made their preferred church the established, or recognized, church of their lands. People who wanted to vote or work in the government had to follow the religion of that church. Madison convinced the representatives to add a law that protected the rights of U.S. citizens to practice any religion. Over time Madison worked to get Thomas Jefferson's Religious Freedom Bill passed. This bill would free Virginia of an established church. In 1786, 10 years later, the bill finally passed.

1

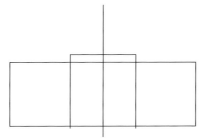

The Virginia Statehouse is where Virginians declared their independence from Great Britain on June 29, 1776. To draw the statehouse, start out with a large horizontal rectangle. Draw a vertical line down the middle of it. Add straight lines as shown.

2

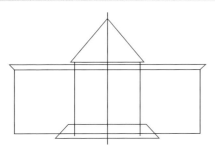

Draw a trapezoid at the bottom of the rectangle as shown. Add a shape that makes a triangle at the top. The vertical line extends through the middle. Add two short slanted lines to either side of the top of the rectangle. Connect them with a horizontal line.

3

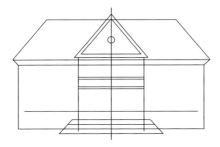

Using straight lines, draw the roof. Draw a smaller triangle inside the triangle from step 2. Add a small circle inside the triangle. Add horizontal lines as shown.

4

Erase extra lines. Add two thin shapes on the roof for chimneys. Add horizontal lines across the base of the roof and to the statehouse as shown. Add vertical lines to the middle. Add rectangles for window as shown. Use slanted lines in the trapezoid for the stairs.

5

Erase extra lines. Add lines to the tops of the columns and chimneys. Add more windows and horizontal lines across the middle of each. Add vertical lines in between the top columns. Add the front door.

6

Erase extra lines including window guides. Add vertical and horizontal lines to the inside of the windows. Shade the statehouse using the tip of your pencil. Notice how some parts are darker than others. Excellent work!

Father of the Constitution

When the American Revolution ended in 1783, the newly independent colonies were governed by the Articles of Confederation. Soon the nation's leaders realized that the articles were not working well. In 1787, Madison and 54 other representatives attended the Constitutional Convention in Philadelphia, Pennsylvania, to fix the problems. They created a new outline for government, which became the Constitution of the United States. The articles had given most of the power to colonial governments, but the Constitution gave most of the power to the national government. Though Madison helped write some of the Constitution, his main efforts went toward convincing representatives who were suspicious of a strong national government to support the Constitution. Thanks to his efforts, the Constitution was finally ratified in 1788. On October 18, 2001, the U.S. Postal Service created a stamp to honor the 250th birthday of James Madison, the Father of the Constitution.

1

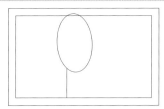

To draw Madison's 2001 postage stamp, start with two large rectangles, one inside the other. Draw a slightly slanted oval for the face as shown. Add a vertical line from the oval to the bottom of the inner rectangle.

2

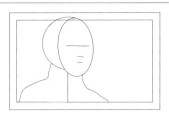

Add a curved line to the left side of the oval. This shape will form the side of the head. Draw curved lines as shown to form the neck and shoulders. Draw three horizontal guidelines in the oval for the face.

3

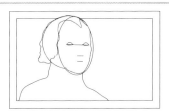

Erase any extra lines. Draw two ovals for the eyes. With a rough line, draw the cheek and jawline using the oval as your guide. Using the half-moon shape and the oval as your guides, draw the hairline and hair.

4

Erase the curved head guide and the line across the eyes. Add a circle in the center of each eye. Draw eyebrows and finish the right side of the hair. Add a ponytail and hair ribbon. Draw his shirt and his jacket's collar.

5

Erase extra lines. Add curved lines and dots to the eyes. Draw the nose, lips, chin, and cheeks. Add ruffles to the shirt and circles for buttons on the coat. Draw horizontal lines in the background. Add a shape on top.

6

Draw small half circles along the inside of the outer rectangle. Erase face guidelines. Add shapes to the building. Write the name "James Madison" as shown. Write "USA" and add the number 34 as shown.

7

Add wavy lines for the hair. Add a small curve to the left eyebrow. Using curved and squiggly lines, add trees to the scene behind Madison. Add lines to the building on the right.

8

Finish James Madison's stamp with shading. Use short lines that cross over each other to shade in the coat. Add as much detail as you like. Well done! Your stamp looks great!

The Federalist Papers and Ratifying the Constitution

After the Constitutional Convention, James Madison worked to convince the new state governments to ratify the Constitution. Two New York politicians, John Jay and Alexander Hamilton, asked for Madison's help in writing 85  papers defending the Constitution. They thought that explaining how the Constitution benefited the people would convince the state governments to ratify it. These papers, the Federalist Papers, appeared in New York newspapers from 1787 to 1788. In one of Madison's better-known essays, he explained that the Constitution would divide the national government into three branches, each with different powers. No one branch would be all powerful, so the country could never become a tyranny, which people feared. New York ratified the Constitution. Madison worked to convince other states as well. The cartoon above appeared in 1788 in a newspaper to celebrate the first 10 states, represented by the columns, to ratify the Constitution.

1 Begin the cartoon by drawing a large rectangle. Now add a narrower and slightly longer rectangle beneath the big one. Draw a vertical line. See how the line goes through the center of the rectangles.

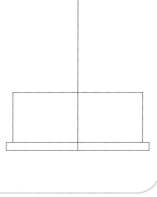

2 Add an arch to the top of the large rectangle as shown. Draw an oval in the center of the arch. The vertical line should go through the center of the oval. Draw two horizontal lines at the bottom of the large rectangle.

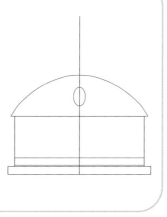

3 Draw two more ovals around the first oval. Add the shapes to the top of the arch. Draw a line across the bottom of the arch. Draw nine long vertical lines and three short ones as guides for the columns.

4 Draw horizontal lines across the base of the rectangle as shown. Draw two arches in the large arch. Draw a stick figure as a guide for the statue. Draw an oval to create the shape of the head.

5 Draw the outline of the statue's dress, leg, and arms. Draw the horn. Add lines to the arch as shown. Draw the first columns using horizontal and vertical lines. Add rectangles to the tops.

6 Erase all extra guidelines. Draw the statue's hair and eye. Add wavy lines to her dress. Add more lines to the base of the arch. Finish the columns and bases using vertical and horizontal lines.

7 Erase the rest of the column guidelines. Erase the oval you used as a guide for the head. Add horizontal and vertical lines to the arch, statue base, and columns as shown. Add lines to the statue's hair and dress.

8 Using the tip of your pencil, add shading to your cartoon. Feel free to shade your own way or use the picture on page 16 to help you. What a great job!

Secretary of State

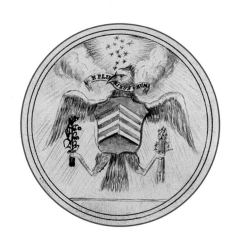

In 1801, Madison became President Jefferson's secretary of state. As secretary, Madison looked after America's foreign affairs. He was also the keeper of the great seal of the United States, an official symbol for America that appeared on papers such as treaties. In 1803, Jefferson bought a stretch of land in midwestern America from France. This was known as the Louisiana Purchase. Some people thought it was unlawful because the Constitution did not clearly state that the president could purchase land. Madison convinced people that it was constitutional. Meanwhile France and England were fighting the Napoleonic Wars. English sailors boarded American ships and forced the American sailors to join their army. Both France and England tried to stop American ships from bringing goods to the other country. Jefferson and Madison passed embargo acts against both countries, hoping to protect American ships and avoid war. Unfortunately, these efforts failed and America went to war with Britain in 1812.

1

You are going to draw the great seal of the United States that Secretary James Madison used. Begin by drawing two circles, one inside the other.

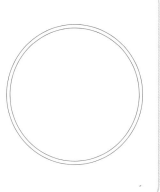

2

Draw a vertical line in the middle of the circle. Add a smaller circle at the tip of the line, slightly off center. These are guidelines for the eagle. Draw the shape for the shield.

3

Add seven upside-down *V*'s to the shield. Line up each point with the vertical line in the center. Using squiggly lines draw feathers on top of the circle. Use wavy lines to draw the neck and the wing on the right.

4

Erase the center line. Add the beak and a line for the eye. Draw the wing on the left. Add a rough line on the top edge of the wing on the right. Draw the tail. Draw one of the legs and claws as shown.

5

Erase the head guide. Add lines to the face, the feathers on the eagle's head, and the wing on the right. Add a rough line to the other wing. Draw the other leg and claw. Add the bundle of arrows as shown.

6

Draw the feathers on the wing on the left and on the tail. Add thin vertical lines to form each arrow. Draw a plant in the claw on the left. With curved and squiggly lines, draw the ribbon in the bird's beak.

7

Write "E PLURIBUS UNUM," which means "from many, one," on the ribbon. Draw 13 stars and a few clouds above the eagle. Add a wreath around the arrows. Draw two horizontal lines at the bottom of the seal.

8

Finish the seal with shading. Lightly shade in the background of the seal using the side of your pencil tip. Darken the feathers and the three stripes on the shield. Shade in the rest as shown. Well done!

President Madison Declares War

On March 4, 1809, James Madison became the fourth president of the United States. Immediately, he struggled to avoid war. Britain continued interfering

with American ships at sea. Madison's patience ran out. Many states wanted war because they believed that Britain was aiding Native American attacks on American settlers. They were also angry with Britain's lack of respect for American sailors and ships. In June 1812, Madison asked for a declaration of war with Britain, and Congress approved it. The War of 1812 had begun.

America was not prepared to fight another war. The army was small and poorly organized. Many of the land battles ended in losses. The navy, however, had a number of great successes. America had few ships, but the ones it had were well made. The *Constitution*, one of America's best ships, won a hard naval battle against the British ship the *Guerrière*. The battle is shown above.

1

Now you are going to learn how to draw the USS *Constitution*. Begin by drawing a wavy line to show the water. Then draw the body of the boat using curved lines as shown.

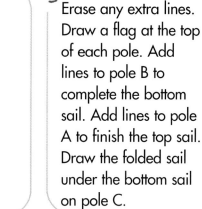

2

Add three vertical poles. We'll call them A, B, and C, from left to right. Notice that the poles are wider at the bottom. Draw the large branchlike shape on the front of the boat as shown.

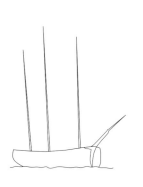

3

Erase any extra lines. Draw horizontal lines. There are two lines on pole C, one line on pole B, and one line across the branchlike shape. Draw a rough triangle for the front sail. Add lines to the front of the boat.

4

Add three lines to form a rectangular shape on the body of the boat. Draw curved and straight lines for two sails on pole C and for the top sail on pole B. Draw a horizontal line across the top of pole A.

5

Erase any extra lines. Draw a flag at the top of each pole. Add lines to pole B to complete the bottom sail. Add lines to pole A to finish the top sail. Draw the folded sail under the bottom sail on pole C.

6

Erase extra lines. Draw a slanted pole with a flag on it extending from pole B. Add lines to the first three flags. Add tiny shapes to the side of the boat. Add lines to the back of the boat.

7

Erase extra lines. Add ropes to the top sails using upside-down V's. Draw another folded sail on pole B. Using slanted lines, add ropes as shown. Add lines to the fourth flag.

8

Finish the USS *Constitution* by shading. Shade in the boat and the left sides of the sails. Add squiggly lines to create the stripes of the American flags. Great job!

Dolley Madison

Dolley Madison was a very active First Lady. In 1809, she organized the first Inaugural Ball in honor of James Madison's presidential election. Dolley started Wednesday Drawing Room evenings, also called Squeezes. Each Wednesday, government officials, politicians, and others were welcomed to the White House for parties. These parties were a chance for people with different ideas and backgrounds to talk with one another. Dolley was more than a hostess of parties. She helped statesmen who disagreed get along with one another, and she made people feel at ease. She was also brave. During the War of 1812, the British took over Washington, D.C., and burned parts of the White House. Madison was away but Dolley saved important papers and paintings from the fire. She helped to make the position of the First Lady what it is today.

1

Begin drawing Dolley Madison with an oval. You will use this as a guide to draw the head and face. Now draw a vertical line extending from the right side of the oval. This will be a guide for the neck and body.

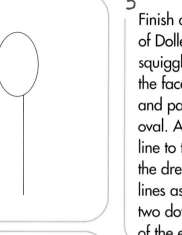

2

Draw a curved shape on the right side of the head oval. Add a slanted oval for the ear at the bottom of the curve. Draw three guidelines inside the oval. Draw guidelines for the shoulders and upper arms as shown.

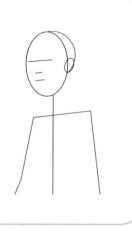

3

Draw small ovals for Dolley's eyes across the top face guideline. Using the lines as your guide, reshape the cheek, the jaw, and the chin. Use curves and wavy lines to form the neck, shoulders, body, and arms.

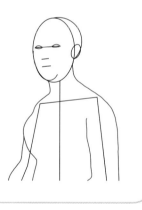

4

Erase the body guidelines and the bottom half of the face oval. Use wavy and squiggly lines to add the hairline. Using the face guides, add the nose and lips. Add eyebrows and small circles in the eyes.

5

Finish drawing the rest of Dolley's hair using squiggly lines. Erase the face guidelines and part of the ear oval. Add a curved line to the ear. Draw the dress using curved lines as shown. Add two dots to the center of the eyes.

6

Erase extra lines. Draw the lace along the dress' edge using squiggly lines. Draw three curved lines on the neck for necklaces. Draw lines as shown around the eyes.

7

Finish your drawing of Dolley with shading. Darken Dolley's hair, the inner circle in her eyes, and her lips. Use the side of your pencil tip to shade in her face and body lightly. You can use your finger to blend her skin. Darken the background of the picture and Dolley's left arm. Dolley looks perfect! Great job.

America's Hero

The War of 1812 was not going well, but Madison was still reelected in 1812. In 1814, Britain finally defeated France and put all its effort into fighting America. However, in September 1814, America had a major victory. Americans discovered the British planned to attack Baltimore, Maryland. American soldiers at Fort McHenry, which guarded

Baltimore's harbor, fought the British and stopped the attack. Francis Scott Key, an American onlooker, wrote the poem "The Star-Spangled Banner" about the battle. It became America's national anthem in 1931. In the above painting, Key looks at the American flag from a boat. By Christmas Eve 1814, both countries were tired of fighting. They ended the war by signing the Treaty of Ghent. Madison had led America into war against a powerful country and had proven America's strength to the world. Madison became a hero.

1 You are going to draw a cannon from Fort McHenry. Draw two slanted vertical lines as shown. Draw a line that crosses over the middle of both lines. These will be guides for the wheels and the body of the cannon.

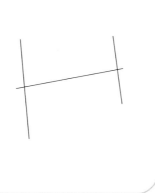

2 Draw an oval around the two vertical lines for the wheels as shown. Draw short, straight lines at the top and the bottom of the left oval. Draw a long, slanted line that touches the top of the right wheel.

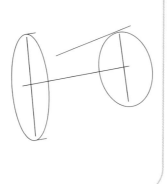

3 Connect the small straight lines on the left oval with an arch that is the same height as the oval. Draw shapes as shown for guides to the cannon's body. Erase the vertical wheel lines from step 1.

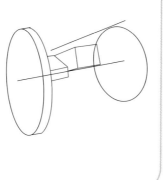

4 Draw an oval on the tip of the cannon guideline. Draw a curved line on the outside of the right wheel. Draw the shapes inside the wheels as shown. Add two lines to the body of the cannon.

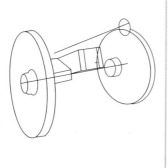

5 Add curved lines to both wheels and an oval inside the left wheel. Draw straight lines under the body of the cannon. Add a small shape to the body. Draw the cannon by adding lines to the guide.

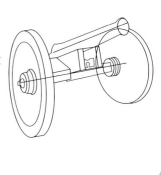

6 Erase the guidelines for the body and the cannon. Draw squiggly shapes on the left side of the cannon body and add small straight lines to the bottom of the cannon's body. Add slanted lines to the wheels.

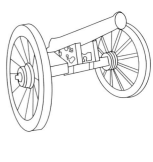

7 Erase any extra lines. Finish the inside of the wheels with more slanted lines. Add shapes around the sides of the wheels as shown. Draw a small oval at the mouth of the cannon.

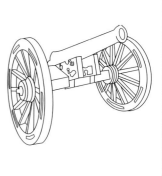

8 Finish the body with shading. Darken the cannon and the rims of both wheels. Shade in some of the lines on the inside of the wheels as well as some of the shapes on the body. Good work!

A Busy Retirement

After finishing his second presidential term in 1817, Madison retired. He moved to Montpelier, his plantation, shown here. He lived the life of a farmer while Dolley continued to host her famous gatherings.

Madison spent much of his time organizing all the papers that he had written during his life, so that later generations could learn from them. He also wrote newspaper articles and advised the new president, James Monroe, on foreign affairs. Madison also wrote his autobiography during his retirement. In 1829, Madison served as one of the leaders of the Virginia Constitutional Convention, a meeting held to consider changes to Virginia's constitution. On June 28, 1836, James Madison died. He had taken good care of himself, because of his health problems. Madison lived to be 85 years old. He was the last of the Founding Fathers to die. He had worked hard all his life for America and had played a major part in the survival of the country.

1

Begin drawing Montpelier with three rectangles. We'll call them A, B, and C, from left to right. Rectangles A and C are the same size. Rectangle B is larger. Rectangle C is slightly higher and is attached to rectangle B.

2

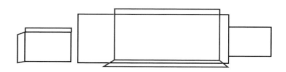

Draw another rectangle, D, over rectangle B. Add a trapezoid to the bottom of rectangle D as shown. Add straight lines to the side and top of the rectangle A.

3

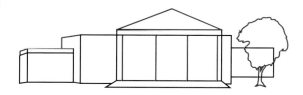

Erase extra lines. Add an upside-down V on top of rectangle D for the roof. Add four vertical lines in rectangle B as guidelines. In front of rectangle C, draw a tree. Add small lines to the left sides of rectangles A and B.

4

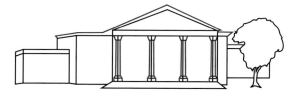

Using the vertical lines as guides, draw the columns as shown. Draw lines along the top of rectangle B, the roof, and rectangle C. Erase the lines from rectangle C that run through the tree.

5

Erase extra lines. Draw the windows and door on rectangle B. Add two more columns to rectangle B as shown. Add another upside-down V to the side of the roof. Draw a chimney on rectangle B's right side.

6

Draw lines inside the trapezoid for the steps. Add more lines to the roof, including two curved lines beneath the triangle. Draw more windows. On top of the door, draw a rectangle with an arch shape on top.

7

Erase extra lines. Draw lines in the windows and on the tops of the columns. Add three more chimneys. Add squares to the tops of rectangles A and C. Draw lines extending from rectangles A and C for the ground.

8

Erase extra lines. Finish Montpelier with shading. Darken the windows, door, and parts of the roof. Lightly shade the building and tree as you wish. Your drawing looks great!

Why Madison Is Important

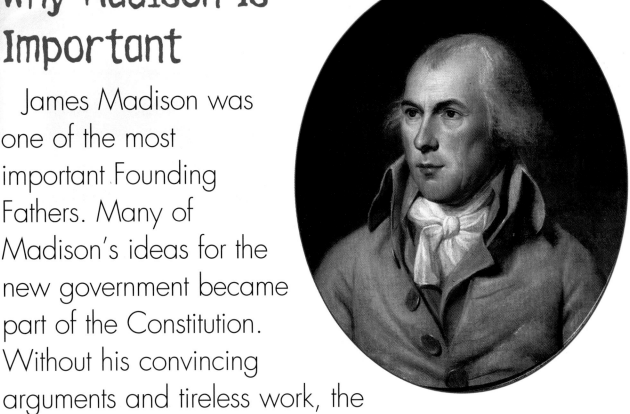

James Madison was one of the most important Founding Fathers. Many of Madison's ideas for the new government became part of the Constitution. Without his convincing arguments and tireless work, the Constitution might never have been ratified by the original states. Madison also led America through the War of 1812, a war that could have easily destroyed the new country. Madison proved to the world that America could not be bullied. Madison's papers helped the people who came after him understand the new government that he had helped create.

Madison was a hardworking, intelligent American. He labored all his life for his country. For his role in writing the Constitution and getting it ratified, he truly earned his nickname, Father of the Constitution.

1 Now you will draw this famous painting of James Madison by Charles Willson Peale. Draw an oval to use as a guide for Madison's head. Draw a vertical line, as shown, as a guideline for the neck.

5 Erase the remaining guidelines. Add small dots in the eyes. Draw more hair as shown. Begin to draw the collar and arm of the coat using wavy lines. Add a curved line to his nose and his chin.

2 Add a curved line to the right side of the oval. Add a slanted oval for the ear. Draw three horizontal lines as guides for the face. Draw three straight guidelines for the shoulders and upper arms as shown.

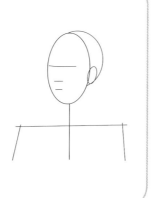

6 Erase extra lines. Draw the collar for the vest beneath the coat using wavy lines. Add two buttons to the left side of the outer coat. Add a line to the jaw as shown.

3 Erase part of the head oval and ear oval as shown. Draw two ovals across the top face guideline for the eyes. Reshape the face using the oval as your guide. Draw the outline of the neck, shoulders, and arms.

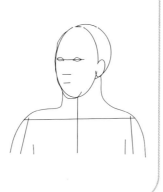

7 Erase the extra lines on the neck that the clothing covers. Draw the bow and lines on the collar of the inner shirt. There is a rough square shape in the middle for the knot.

4 Erase extra lines as shown. Draw the hairline using wavy lines. Add the eyebrows. Add *U* shapes inside the eyes. Use the two other face guidelines to add the nose and mouth.

8 Erase any extra lines. Finish your drawing of Madison with shading. Use the side of your pencil tip to lightly shade the head. Notice that the eyebrows and parts of the collars are very dark. He looks great!

Timeline

1751 James Madison is born on March 16.

1769 Madison goes to college in New Jersey, at what is now known as Princeton University.

1772 Madison leaves school and goes back to Virginia.

1775 The American Revolution begins.

1776 Madison attends the Virginia Convention in Williamsburg.

1783 The American Revolution ends. The colonies are governed by the Articles of Confederation.

1787 Madison attends the Constitutional Convention in Philadelphia, Pennsylvania, where the U.S. Constitution is created.

1787 Madison aids Alexander Hamilton and John Jay in writing the Federalist Papers.

1801 Madison becomes President Jefferson's secretary of state.

1803 Jefferson purchases land from France. This deal is known as the Louisiana Purchase.

1809 Madison is inaugurated as president of the United States on March 4.

1812 The War of 1812 begins. The USS *Constitution* defeats the British *Guerrière*. Madison is reelected as president.

1814 Americans fight the British at Fort McHenry. Francis Scott Key writes "The Star-Spangled Banner."

1817 Madison retires to Montpelier.

1829 Madison attends the Virginia Constitutional Convention.

1836 James Madison dies on June 28, at the age of 85.

Glossary

American Revolution (uh-MER-uh-ken reh-vuh-LOO-shun) Battles that soldiers from the colonies fought against Britain for freedom, from 1775 to 1783.

anthem (AN-thum) A blessed or an official song.

Articles of Confederation (AR-tih-kulz UV kun-feh-deh-RAY-shun) The laws that governed the United States before the Constitution was created.

autobiography (ah-toh-by-AH-gruh-fee) The story of a person's life written by that person.

Christianity (kris-chee-A-nih-tee) A faith based on the teachings of Jesus Christ and the Bible.

Constitution (kon-stih-TOO-shun) The basic rules by which the United States is governed.

Constitutional Convention (kon-stih-TOO-shuh-nul kun-VEN-shun) The political body that met in the summer of 1787 to create the U.S. Constitution.

declared (dih-KLAYRD) Announced officially.

dedicated (DEH-dih-kayt-ed) Gave to a purpose.

defeated (dih-FEET-ed) Won against someone in a contest or battle.

defending (dih-FEND-ing) Taking someone's side in an argument.

embargo (im-BAR-go) Order forbidding business or other activity.

foreign affairs (FOR-in uh-FAYRZ) Dealings with other countries.

Founding Fathers (FOWND-ing FAH-therz) The men who formed the government of the United States.

inaugurated (ih-NAW-gyuh-rayt-ed) Swore in a government official.

information (in-fer-MAY-shun) Knowledge or facts.

involved (in-VOLVD) Kept busy by something.

plantation (plan-TAY-shun) A very large farm where crops were grown.

politicians (pah-lih-TIH-shunz) People who hold or run for a public office.

ratified (RA-tih-fyd) Approved or agreed to something in an official way.

restored (rih-STORD) Put back; returned to an earlier state.

survival (sur-VY-val) Staying alive.

symbol (SIM-bul) An object or a picture that stands for something else.

tyranny (TEER-uh-nee) A government in which one ruler has all the power.

Index

Web Sites

Due to the changing nature of Internet links, PowerKids Press has developed an online list of Web sites related to the subject of this book. This site is updated regularly. Please use this link to access the list:
www.powerkidslinks.com/kgdpusa/madison/